Adobe Architecture

by Myrtle & Wilfred Stedman

the sunstone press

Santa Fe, New Mexico / 1973

FIRST EDITION

PRINTING HISTORY

Santa Fe Style Homes: Eighteen Interpretative Designs by Wilfred H. Stedman was published in 1936 by Santa Fe Builders Supply Company.
"How To Make An Horno" by Myrtle Stedman appeared in *New Mexico Magazine,* August, 1969.
These sections are reprinted here by permission.

Library of Congress Catalog No.: 73-77322
ISBN *0-913270-12-1*

Printed in the United States of America
Printed by Starline, Albuquerque, New Mexico

With love, to our two sons, Thomas Wilfred and Wilfred Donald, who apply their own individual artistic and creative capabilities to the fields of electronics and orthopedic surgery, respectively.

Adobe Architecture

ACKNOWLEDGMENTS

To John Walter who, at the time of initial publication of a book called *Santa Fe Style Homes,* was Executive Vice President of Santa Fe Builders Supply Company, the company who sponsored the book. Mr. Walter instigated the book's birth and in doing so gave much pleasure to interested builders and of course made this publication possible.

To the *New Mexico Magazine,* a publication whose aims and interests are closely related to the craftsmen of New Mexico. An article by Mrs. Stedman was published in the August issue, 1969, "How To Make An Horno."

To John David Concha and to Eva Concha (Taos Pueblo) for their helpful and careful instructions and actual demonstration given to Mrs. Stedman about their skill in the art of adobe making. And to Alma Concha (Taos Pueblo) for her recipe for Indian bread and the necessary "pointers" which create the delicious kind of bread she makes.

To the Tesuque Home Builders Crew, a very special thanks. These people are both neighbors and workers, all experts in adobe.

The Origin of Santa Fe Style Architecture

Centuries ago there existed throughout the Southwest, even as now, Indian races highly developed and skillful in the art of building. Surviving Indian Pueblos, visible today, have changed little since the time of their development. It is largely to these unique and indigenous apartment houses that we owe our present day architecture known as Santa Fe Style. The Spanish colonists entering this country in the 16th century brought the faith, culture, customs and architecture of Spain. But adjustment to climatic conditions, use of local material and employment of native craftsmen effected marked changes, creating an architecture peculiar to the Southwest. The beauty and charm of this Santa Fe Style depends entirely upon sincerity and simplicity, the organic character of structural design being allowed expression according to its function. The large Spanish homes were usually built to enclose a patio in which the family life centered; here, screened from public gaze, were gay "mecetas", flowering shrubs, birds — a pool or well, bright colors, shade, comfort. Certain designs herein incorporate this feature in a modified way. It is not our intention to show the pretentious, but to depict modest designs suitable to modern requirements, compact in arrangement and fitting the limited area of the average building lot. We hope this volume may be helpful, and an incentive in perpetuating Santa Fe Style architecture in its beauty and simplicity.

WILFRED STEDMAN

Casita Pequena

An attractive house . . . small yet commodious and easy to manage; ample closet space, large living room — a portal — a walled garden space. Another bedroom can easily be added later on, either at front or rear, the complete unit suitable for the smaller building lot.

FOUNDATIONS Adequate foundations insure uniform distribution of a building's weight on the soil, preventing settlement and cracking of walls, reducing maintenance and prolonging the life of the structure. Concrete foundations are best, being proof against freezing and thawing, economical and permanent. Where the ground is firm, a clean trench may be dug to receive concrete, forms being required only above grade. Adobe walls weigh about 115 pounds per cubic foot; the dead load of an adobe house is therefore rather high, and the material of a nature requiring absolute protection from surface water. Concrete foundations should be carried above grade at least six inches, the surface soil pitched to shed water away from walls and footings. The foundation must be at least as wide as the adobe wall and deep enough to be below frost line and to reach good bearing soil free of humus. Soft clays or loams, undisturbed by laborers' tools, will carry approximately one ton per square foot, while gravelly soils and hard clays will carry as high as five tons per square foot: an examination into the type of soil on the site is therefore advisable.

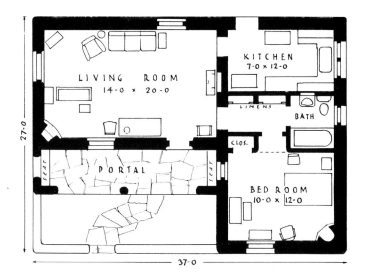

2

The Studio Guest House

An arrangement very suitable for guests, or a resident couple; the main room large enough to combine living room and work room, while a studio couch would accommodate another individual. The built-in garage, accessible in any weather, is an added attraction and affords the "handyman" a convenient workshop.

ADOBE STRUCTURES Sun-dried mud bricks have been the common building material used in arid countries through the ages. Well puddled mud, mixed with straw to prevent undue cracking in the drying, makes a building material worthy of respect. Adobe buildings are permanent if properly designed and constructed with ample foundations, and walls protected from the capillary action of ground water and consequent erosion. These houses are cool in summer, easily heated in winter. The labor for making bricks and laying them is plentiful and material for brickmaking usually can be found on the site. Average adobe possesses an ultimate compressive strength of about 400 pounds per square inch; a safety factor of six permits a working strength of about 67 pounds per square inch. Care must be taken that no stress exceeds this limit. Vigas must rest on adequate plates, distributing loads without eccentricity. Corners must be strong; the space between an outside corner and nearest opening should be greater than the width of such opening; wall abutments are sometimes needed for extra strength.

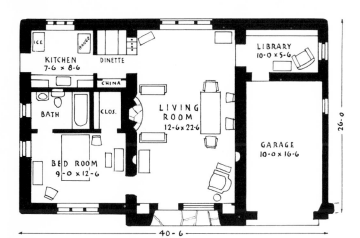

WILFRED STEDMAN

For the Small Family

A suitable design for a small family; compact and convenient, saving area by dispensing with dining room and serving meals in the dinette, or outdoors in patio, weather permitting. Cost estimates cannot be given here, inasmuch as costs are dependent upon labor charges, location and the general finish chosen by the owners.

FIREPLACES The fireplaces appropriate for these homes are invariably simple, their beauty dependent upon tapering lines and sound proportions. Handsome as the native fireplace is, it generally smokes and here we find room for improvement. To draw properly, and be unaffected by contrary winds, a fireplace must be built with smoke chamber and baffle shelf to deflect the downdraft up and out of chimney. The flue and throat, while different in shape, must be alike in area and this area must not be less than 1/12 of the fireplace opening. Sides of fireplace must be vertical to the throat, which is full width of the fireplace opening. The underside of this long narrow throat is set about 8 inches above the lintel soffit and back from fireplace breast about 4 inches. A diagram is shown on page 13. Metal throats with hinged dampers are available in various sizes, assuring proper construction and conserving heat; these dampers are adjustable. Fireplaces should be built only by those with experience in this work, to insure an owner the comfort and cheer a good fireplace affords; when improperly constructed the fault can rarely ever be remedied later.

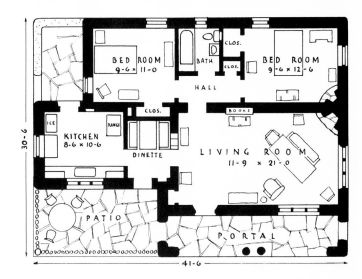

WILFRED STEDMAN

WILFRED STEDMAN

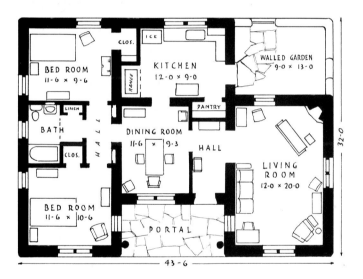

CLOS.

ICE

WALLED GARDEN
9-0 × 13-0

BED ROOM
11-6 × 9-6

KITCHEN
12-0 × 9-0

RANGE

LINEN

PANTRY

BATH

CLOS.

HALL

DINING ROOM
11-6 × 9-3

HALL

LIVING
ROOM
12-0 × 20-0

32-0

BED ROOM
11-6 × 10-6

PORTAL

43-6

W.S.

The Garden View

Houses should be attractive on all sides, with gardens rather than "back-yards". The planting of trees and shrubs, their enclosure with walls or cedar posts, can create beauty spots which repay their owners in health and happiness. Be careful to keep all planting well away from walls and foundations to prevent upheaval by roots.

ROOFS   There can be no valid objection to flat roofs when properly built — the roofs of practically all large buildings on this continent are of this particular type. These roofs are known as the "built-up" kind, various materials being used in their construction, namely, roofing felts and asphalt, pitch, tar and crude-oil products, or combinations of these materials. Generally, the roof proper is laid upon a smoothly and tightly laid wood surface, usually built with a slight slope to shed the surface water to the canales or downspouts. This type of roof when properly constructed, is as satisfactory and permanent as a roof may be; several nationally known roofing products, tested and approved, are in general use and available in your community. Roofs of this kind are generally topped with coarse gravel imbedded in a flood coat of asphalt or tar. They may be laid directly over dirt insulation properly tamped and graded for drainage. In some cases the dirt insulation is applied directly over the ceiling boards or saplings and under the roof deck. Have your roofing done by an experienced roofer properly equipped.

5

WILFRED STEDMAN

Built-In Garage

The garage can be harmoniously worked into the general design, offering added convenience and shielding the patio from cold winds. The future may see such a garage inexpensively made into an additional room according to requirements.

FLOORS Floors are many and various. Whatever kind is chosen, according to purse and fancy, must have adequate support; see that all beams, joists and sub-flooring, where used, are of proper size and spacing, well blocked and securely nailed. It must be level and even, or furniture receives undue strain; it must be tight, harboring no dirt or vermin; it should be easily cared for; and finally it can be handsome. There are concrete, tile, composition, brick, soft and hard woods, rubber and linoleum to select from, and maintenance and appearance must enter the question of choice. A floor with movable covering is commendable, easily cleaned and allowing changes in rug arrangement. Space does not permit a treatise on floors; advice may be had from any dealer who will gladly show samples and quote prices.

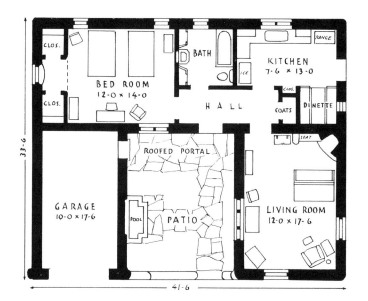

W.S.

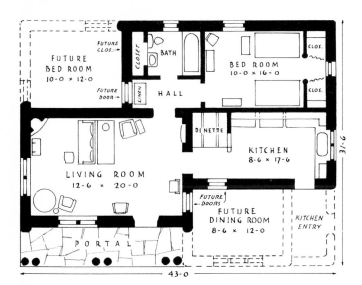

The Modern Kitchen

The kitchen may contain the latest labor-saving devices and yet retain its Southwest flavor. Washable walls, enameled cabinets, sparkling metal and easy-to-clean floors are feasible and practical in the Santa Fe Style homes of the modern-minded.

WINDOWS The massive quality of Santa Fe Style can easily be lost by the use of too many or too large openings. Windows may be smaller in this sunny region; glare inside the home destroys its quiet and repose. The Spanish people shut out sun and heat, having few windows and those small; bright interiors are obtained with use of pale-tinted calcimines or wall paints which reflect light. Window and door frames are best built into place as walls go up, securely anchored there by means of nailing blocks laid in brick joints, in order to withstand weather and repeated slamming. Where window sash are used, bottom rails and sills must be constructed so as to permit no entry of water from rain or melting snow by capillary action; water seeping in at these places will quickly ruin woodwork and wall finish at window stools.

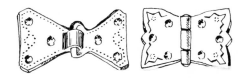

WILFRED STEDMAN

CABINET WORK

Almost every house, however unpretentious, requires a few special cabinets. These can be made up in a mill shop, where they have the tools and trained men to do this type of work, and put into place when completed and delivered. The shop will need drawings or illustrations and specific measurements of the spaces the cabinets are to occupy.

With a Dining Room

Some families place much importance upon a dining room, and consequently this house possesses one, with recess for a built-in sideboard placed conveniently aside to take no floor space. Connecting with the commodious living room, the dining room tends to facilitate entertainment. The hall and coat closet provide for disposal of cloaks for family or visitors. Ample space is allowed around the big fireplace for a group of loquacious friends, assuring comfort and cheer in the winter evenings. If required, a second bedroom may be added, as shown on the plan, the complete unit making a home that is desirable and convenient in its entire arrangement.

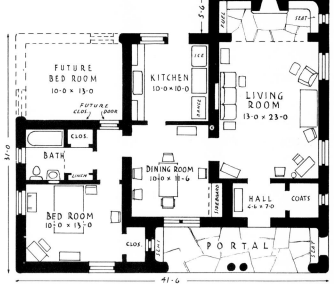

WILFRED STEDMAN

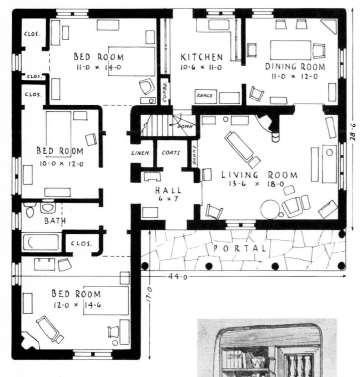

BED ROOM
11-0 × 14-0

KITCHEN
10-6 × 11-0

DINING ROOM
11-0 × 12-0

CLOS.

CLOS.

CLOS.

CUPBD.

RANGE

DOWN

BED ROOM
10-0 × 12-0

LINEN   COATS

LIVING ROOM
13-6 × 18-0

HALL
6 × 7

BATH

CLOS.

PORTAL

44-0

17-0

28-6

BED ROOM
12-0 × 14-6

Central Heating

The larger homes should have provision for a central heating plant, assuring uniform temperatures and abundance of hot water at all times. This house is designed with small basement for this purpose, available from kitchen, with outside fuel-chute at north wall to service the heater. Modern heaters, burning gas or fuel-oil, clean and self regulating, are desirable where conditions permit, and self-feeding coal burners are also available to provide heat with a minimum of labor. The type of heating chosen will require close study so that no mistake will be made in selecting a method of heating which will insure comfort and economical operation.

BUILT-IN FEATURES

The thick adobe walls of these houses permit wall cabinets to be conveniently built-in and floor space conserved. They should be simple in design and well proportioned — an enhancement to the room, serving a definite and useful purpose in the scheme of things.

9

WILFRED STEDMAN

Planned for Greater Convenience

In this design provision is made for a ground floor heating plant, and the garage incorporated into the plan serving as a wind break. A central hall with skylight gives access to main rooms, the heating plant and the rear.

PLASTERING The simplest and least expensive finish for adobe walls is a two-coat plastering of adobe mud. The adobe should be screened free of large gravel and properly tempered with fine sand and the work done by competent men. In arid climates, exposed adobe will weather away about one inch in ten years, necessitating renewal of exterior finish every few years. A permanent exterior finish can be obtained by use of cement plaster, three coats, applied over metal mesh. Inside lime plasters are best applied over metal mesh, also. The mesh must be well nailed to adobe walls or tied to same with loop wires placed in brick courses as walls are laid, the projecting wire ends twisted around the metal mesh. Cement stuccos will never adhere to unprepared adobe walls due to different expansion ratios of adobe and stucco. Adobe plaster cannot be made weather proof by admixture of other materials.

10

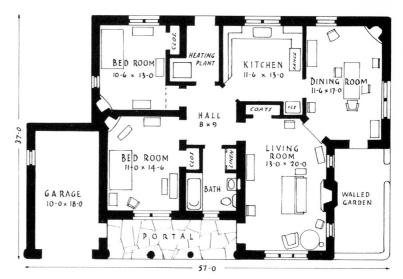

BED ROOM
10-6 × 13-0

HEATING PLANT

KITCHEN
11-6 × 13-0

RANGE

DINING ROOM
11-6 × 17-0

HALL
8 × 9

COATS

ICE

BED ROOM
11-0 × 14-6

CLOS.

LINEN

LIVING ROOM
13-0 × 20-0

GARAGE
10-0 × 18-0

BATH

WALLED GARDEN

PORTAL

37-0

57-0

Some Suggestions for Santa Fe Style Homes

Space permits only a few of the many features possible in these homes. However, let frugality be your guide in this respect and let not a liking for quaintness dull your judgment. Leave plenty of unbroken wall space for that restful quality so essential to livability.

A. Here are two fireplace designs, pleasing for their simplicity of line, and truly native in character.

B. Examples of Spanish lighting fixtures, inexpensive and appropriate, available in a multitude of shapes for walls, ceilings, or tables.

C. A kitchen with built-in cabinets, simple and practical. The louvred doors give access to the sink trap and conceal refuse containers. With judicious use of color, one's kitchen may be a beauty spot — a joy to possess and convenient to use.

D. This sketch shows a dinette in Spanish design, movable for variations in arrangement. Honest and sturdy in construction, these pieces acquire beauty with use and wear.

E. A bookcase, open, built into heavy wall with the Concha motive worked from plastic material or in wood and not too accurate and precise in its finish.

11

Two Small but Liveable Homes

The designs shown here and on page 13 have been arranged for the small family and though compact are roomy and convenient. This style of construction requires a minimum of maintenance, justifying the slightly higher original costs.

THE SPANISH-COLONIAL HOUSE

Santa Fe Style architecture has a close relative, which we now introduce, and for sake of clarity rather than accuracy, this style is termed Spanish-Colonial. The American Occupation of the Southwest saw trained carpenters and masons come into the country; saw-mills operated, brick kilns established. A desire for better houses requiring less maintenance brought about marked changes and improvements in construction. Kiln-burned brick and milled woodwork, paints and varnishes, lime plastered walls became evident, so that the Pueblo quality was lost to these newer creations, though a new beauty and style was founded. The marked differences are many and readily seen. Plastered walls are surmounted with kiln-burned brick cornices, laid in mortar, providing permanent protection to exterior walls. Fireplace backs, hearths and breasts are usually of brick with mantels of wood. Brick is also used extensively in portal floors, door and window sills, while kitchens and bathrooms are floored with tile.

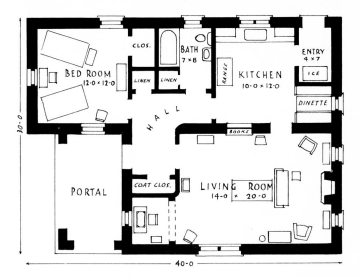

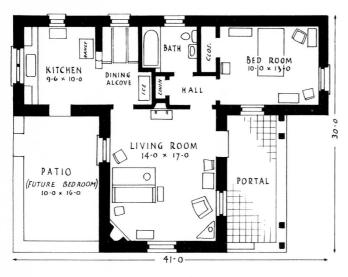

THE SPANISH-COLONIAL (cont.)

Cased openings and architraves are the rule, vigas are milled and rectangular, ceilings are tightly built of tongue and grooved wood, plain or beaded. Roof water is conveyed to the ground or to cisterns by way of metal downspouts with ornamental heads at roof line. The portals are supported on slender pilasters of wood with simple capitals and neck moulds. Windows are equipped with sliding sash and the deep reveals sometimes panelled in wood; hinged shutters at window openings replace the iron or wooden grills. The Spanish-Colonial Style possesses great dignity, its low, long lines suggestive of peace and serenity, a charming architectural style deserving its increasing popularity and importance.

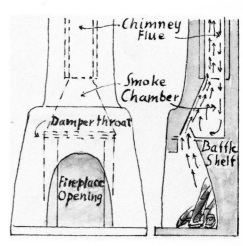

WILFRED STEDMAN

Painting

Paints provide a protective covering for almost any surface, being made for many purposes and of a great number of materials. Paints are available for waterproofing of cement, plaster and similar materials, for reflection or absorption of light, for proof against wear, rot and decay and for purposes of interior decoration as well. Interior woodwork in Santa Fe Style and Old Mexican homes may be painted, but generally is treated with oils, stains and waxes, though all outside surface of frames, sash, casements or doors should be painted or properly treated with varnish or oil to be protected from weather and to prevent warping, swelling and sticking at frames. The woodwork throughout Spanish-Colonial homes should be painted, excepting vigas, which may be stained. All painting of whatever sort should be carefully done in accordance with specifications provided with standard materials for interior and exterior finishes. Wood shrinkage opens up minute cavities where water may enter to break down the protective coating of paint; nail holes and cracks must be puttied, knots shellacked before priming and the work well done to insure the woodwork long life.

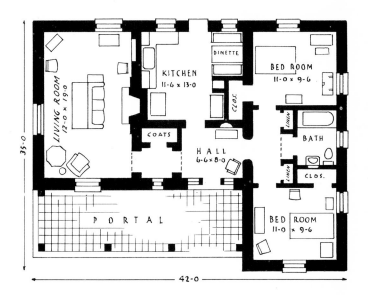

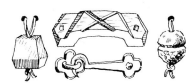

14

The Homelike Dwelling

The home shown here has a touch of the high country in that it has a partial peaked metal roof. It is essentially homelike, while formal and correct. The Spanish-Colonial architecture is obviously of a practical order; it requires that decorative schemes be in strict harmony. Interiors should be bright and cheerful; only light tints and colors used, warm or cool schemes as the various rooms may require. Furnishings should be carefully chosen for utility, comfort and appearance so they fit into the decorative scheme. Landscaping should also be of the formal kind, a balanced arrangement rather than a symetrical one; brick edged pools, walled or sunken gardens, arbors, all enter the spirit of this period. The building of a home, the selection of its style and method of construction, costs of maintenance and other matters require considerable study and sometimes the advice of those qualified by experience. One must go into the many questions involved imbued with the thought that their solution must result in a home meeting fully the family's requirements, the family's financial budget, and that it be handsome and permanent. Inexpensive materials can be used to advantage. Lower grade oak flooring, for instance, costs less than first grade pine, resulting in a hard wood floor showing interesting whorls and color variations. A home will generally succeed in reflecting the character and personality of its owner and be an outward indication of the owner's circumstances and taste for the artistic.

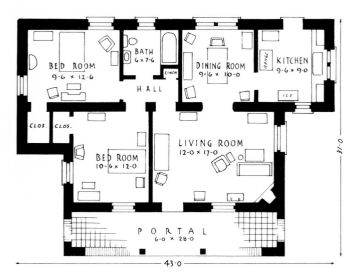

WILFRED STEDMAN

For the Larger Family

Because additional rooms are ofttimes needed, this house is arranged so that a third bedroom may, if desired, be substituted in place of a garage, at time of building or left to the future. This space is large enough to provide a bedroom and heating room accessible from living room, in which case the garage would be placed elsewhere on the site. The exterior and interiors are simple and dignified, a house which will grow old gracefully and always in good taste.

STOCK FIXTURES Many devices are available to make housekeeping easier and homes more efficient. Prospective home owners will do well to acquaint themselves with the many innovations now procurable for the comfort and operation of the modern home. To those who are not in sympathy with the house built of adobe, we wish to state that the architectural designs in this volume may be carried out satisfactorily with other materials; namely, hollow tile or brick construction. Many Santa Fe Style homes are built thus, and the curves and roundings may be built into the masonry. The straight lines and crisp edges of the Spanish-Colonial Style are naturally resultant from truly built masonry, adobe or otherwise, so that these unusual and altogether charming homes may be constructed of burned clay products in any climate, in any part of America, and in accordance with civic building codes.

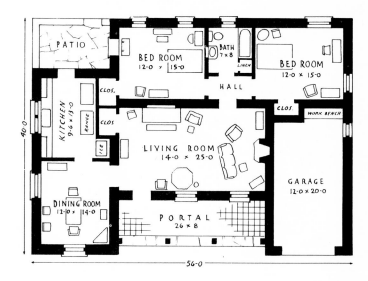

A Few Ideas for Interiors

The possibilities for creating decorative and useful features in the home are endless. We can show but a few of these and recommend that features of this order be placed only where there is a very good reason for their existence. Usually these simple features can be carried out by carpenters at no great cost.

A. A built-in secretary and book case, recessed into an inside adobe wall, very ornamental and practical.

B. A wall niche, shelved and decorated, to house bric-a-brac, or ornamental utensils of the kitchen or pantry.

C. This sketch shows a large window with seat and hinged grille concealing a heat radiator, allowing heat to rise and remove the chill always created by a large area of glass, particularly a north studio-light.

D. Two types of fireplace in Spanish-Colonial design, with brick hearths and openings and wood mantels and casing.

E. Spanish style lighting fixtures of tin, cunningly handmade and obtainable in a great variety of shapes and sizes, and for varied purposes. Sometimes combined with mirrors, plaques and frames, these quaint fixtures are an essential part of the decorative scheme and impart that truly Spanish flavor throughout the home.

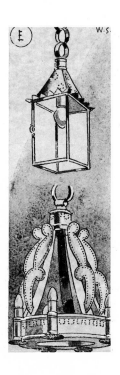

Reminiscent of Old Mexico

In addition to Santa Fe Style and Spanish-Colonial architecture, we must not neglect the architectural achievement of Old Mexico, a style which also belongs in the Southwest, appropriate and beautiful. More and more, houses in this delightful manner will be built hereabout in the near future, the buff and orange colored tile roofs blending harmoniously with the surroundings and the prevailing Santa Fe Style. Again, simplicity is the keynote, and where colors are used, they are used with taste and restraint. Construction is that of the typical adobe building, the projecting vigas roofed over to their ends, forming wide eaves and protecting the walls. Sometimes this method is varied, the roof tiles set in close to the walls allowing but a few inches for a drip, particularly at gables. Interiors, while simple, usually boast of patterned tile used as wainscots, architraves and worked into sink-backs, patios and pools. Potted flowers and cacti on window stools and in patios lend color to these picturesque casas of Spanish origin. Wrought iron is liberally used but always for a purpose and always handsome. Prospective home builders will do well to familiarize themselves with this style of architecture, a style which is so intriguing that we are at a loss to understand why it has hitherto been more or less neglected outside of Old Mexico. It is a distinctive style deserving of consideration by those contemplating new homes in any locality.

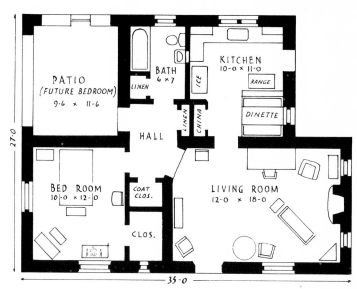

18

The Enclosed Patio

We could not resist showing at least one design with secluded patio, small as it may be. With potted flowers and plants and gay colored table and chairs, even a small patio is well worthwhile and, sheltered as this one is, soon becomes the favored lounging place through the warm weather, a place for cool drinks and snacks, friends and entertainment.

PLUMBING AND WIRING Building codes generally govern sanitation methods, the running of water and soil pipe, and proper ventilation of fixtures. Septic tanks, where used are also regulated by health measures, and a reliable plumbing contractor will shoulder all these technical details. However, the life of the sanitary system depends upon best quality materials being purchased by owner. Electrical work likewise is regulated by codes; employ only a reputable contracting firm. Provide for plenty of electric plugs and outlets, cost of same being small at time of construction, but more costly if added after roughing-in work has been completed.

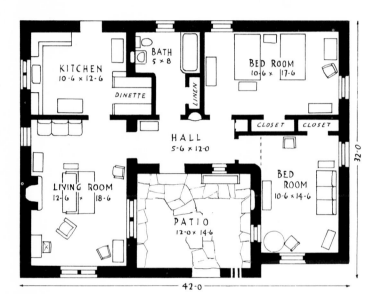

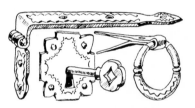

In the Old Mexican Style

Houses built in this manner will be slightly higher in cost, because of tile roof construction. However, Spanish roof tiles are now being made in this region and costs have consequently decreased. Roofs of this type are truly permanent, but necessitate an under-roof of wood sheathing and roll roofing, excepting patios and portals where the tiling may be laid on wood slats carried across rafters, the under side of tiles exposed to view. Metal rain troughs and conductors should be used where a drip would be objectionable or destructive. An insulation of about three inches of screened dirt, covering top of wood ceiling sheathing, will keep out summer heat and retain warmth during winter. Chimney tops are made ornate with brick or tile, triangular vents worked into the pattern and the whole capped with brick or flag stone. Informal planting and a lavish use of jardiniers and flowerpots, rock and cacti gardens, will carry out the colorful outdoor quality needed. Decorative tile interior trimmings are used sparingly or lavishly according to taste, and patios and certain inside floors may be paved with tile of the large plain vitrified kind, laid up in cement upon a concrete slab poured on the ground. A very little decorative tiling judiciously placed will create the desired Old Mexican atmosphere, so tile should be used only where there is a practical need for it, and well chosen.

Homes for Larger Families

These two pages show designs of the more pretentious order, of six and seven rooms. The illustration on page 20 shows a house built around a small enclosed flag-stoned patio, roofed over and illuminated with a skylight of glass which admits all the beneficial sun rays. This patio, a place for colorful plants and flowers, for reading table and easy chairs; conveniently accessible to all main rooms, it serves a dual purpose. The house shown on this page introduces the squat, round columns at portal so typical of the Old Mexican period. This house, too, is commodious and provides space for a central heater, a feature which should be incorporated in all the larger homes. Generally the heating plant is best placed in a small basement, thereby utilizing gravity to speed circulation, whether hot-air, hot-water, gas or steam heat is to be used for heating. Rooms are all large and the portal will accommodate table and deck chairs for al fresco occasions. The sketch shows a house adapting itself to an irregular site, the floors being at slightly different levels, making interiors interesting and native in character; the exterior of the house appears to grow out of the ground and become an integral part of the site and landscape. Walls of bathrooms and kitchens may be finished in various ways with new tile-like materials, washable and durable, creating effects that are sanitary and practical.

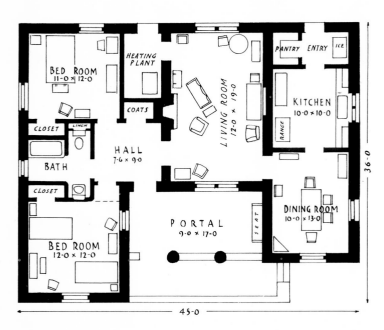

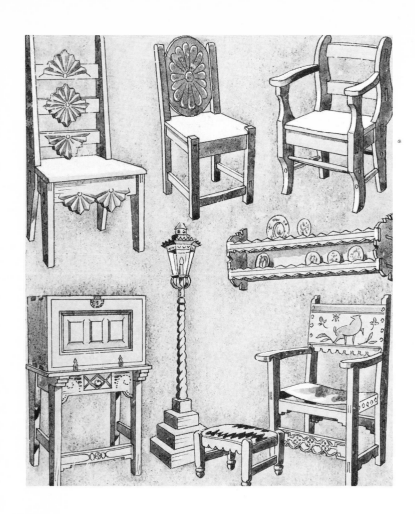

Furniture

This page, showing furniture contemporary with this Southwest period of architecture, can hardly begin to show the great variety in their respective kinds. These examples are typical, however, of the furniture made by the Spanish-Colonial influence. Native soft pine was used almost exclusively, the chamfered edges and gentle wear-curves resulting therefrom, and the designs were more massive than if hardwoods had been available. Spanish homes were sparsely furnished, little else but tables, chairs, beds, chests and trasteros being required, but these were made in an infinite variety of designs, all simple and sturdy, well suited to their function. The surface finish is simple, consisting mostly of clay stains treated with oils and waxes, the pieces taking on a patina with usage. Hand-made furniture of this kind is readily available, or made to order, in the city of Santa Fe and in this region. Your dealer will gladly cooperate to secure the proper furniture and millwork needed for your new home.

WILFRED STEDMAN

A Few Features

The suggestions on this page are not all essential, some being purely decorative extravagances.

A. A patio or garden entrance which can be widened to accommodate cars, if desired.

B. Wood gates to walled gardens or patios.

C. Types of corbel used to decrease long spans for vigas.

D. Two commonly used types of canale, carrying roof water away from foundations. These should be lined with metal or asphalt.

E. Grilles of wood or iron enhance and guard a window opening.

F. A Colonial type of fan-light over a main entrance way.

G. Two kinds of brick coping with dentil courses as used on Spanish-Colonial houses.

H. Doors suitable to the various styles of home depicted herein; the two on left of stock design.

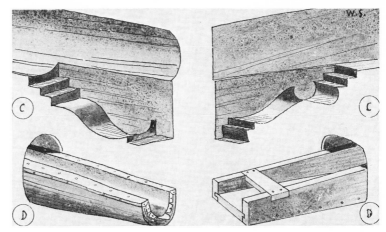

Construction Details

To make this volume more complete, we present here a few drawings showing approved and tested methods of construction in general use throughout the Southwest for Santa Fe Style homes. Thrift in building is always commendable, but beware of savings that mean skimpy construction, savings that react to cause future losses and irreparable damage — the jerry-built house is an abomination. Guard against shoddy workmanship and materials; the savings effected, if any, are small and always prove to be very regrettable. The best is cheapest in the end and the pride of possession, the enjoyment of a well-built lasting home, is beyond price. New materials and methods of construction are constantly being developed, and we cannot in this book cover these many phases, but urge that you visit the display room of dealers in your immediate vicinity. It is hoped that this has been of assistance in the planning or remodeling of homes and an inspiration toward the future expansion and adaptation of the styles and means presented.

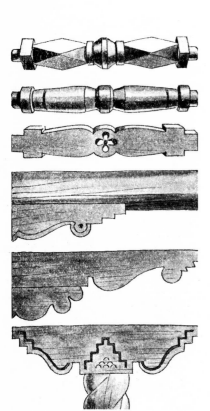

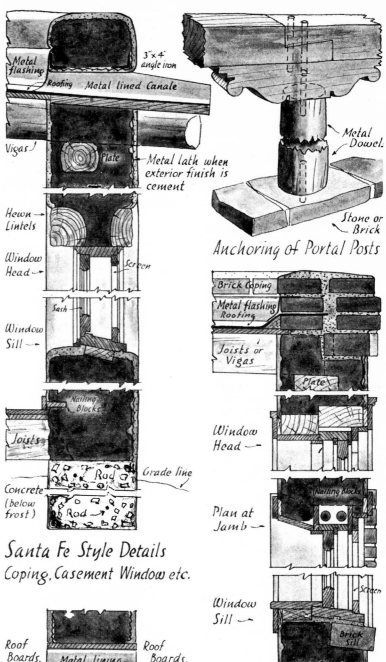

Anchoring of Portal Posts

Santa Fe Style Details
Coping, Casement Window etc.

Detail of Roof Scupper

Spanish Colonial Details
Coping, Double-hung Window

Ceiling Detail (Saplings or Cedar)

24

Making Adobes

There are tradesmen who make adobes by the thousands and will deliver cured ones to your building site, but it is the purpose of this section to give information about how an experienced adobe man and two helpers may go about making adobes in a traditional manner. That is, making them ahead of the actual building schedule, after the frosts in a month when there is little rain, lots of sun and wind and by using the soil on site or bringing it in. Too much sand causes crumbling, too much clay shrinkage. The adobe maker in the illustration has found his ground just right. He has spaded up an area 8 or 10 feet in diameter, made a mound of the spaded dirt, made a crater in his mound, added the second ingredient, water, and let it soak for the night. In the morning he sprinkles chopped straw over the saturated adobe. His helpers are preparing to tromp the straw into the adobe and turn it with their shovels until all is thoroughly mixed and ready to be poured into brick form.

25

A young passerby has stopped and is giving
the adobe maker a hand in clearing an area
of grass and weeds, making ready a place to
mold the adobes. The ground is soft enough
to be smoothed out with the back of the
rake so that he will have a clean flat surface
on which to place the adobes. The grass and
weeds are last year's growth so that there is
not too much work involved. The adobe
maker notes the slope of the ground and will
lay, rack and stack his adobes in rows fol-
lowing the slope downhill for proper drainage. He will be careful where he places his
stacks so that they will be conveniently lo-
cated but not in his way when he starts to
build. The adobes can remain in the stack
until they are removed to be laid in the walls
of his house. He is fortunate to have plenty
of room near his pit for both making and
stacking, and he has plenty of room to get a
truck in should he need to bring in either
sand or clay. His irrigation ditch will supply
him with water. Otherwise, he would have to
have water from another source or haul it in.
Besides three shovels, a pick, an axe and
some straw that he has already used, plus the
hoe and rake he is using, he will need a sturdy wheelbarrow, an adobe form (for size and
shape in general use see illustration), a tub,

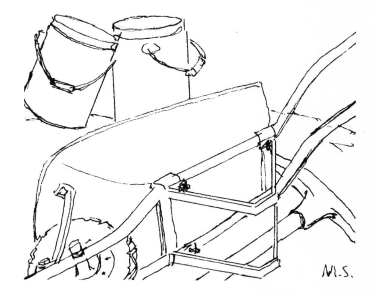

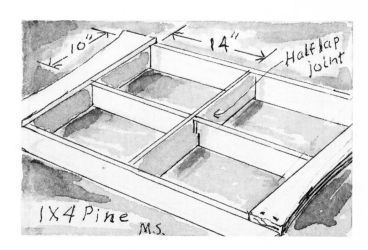

26

M.S.

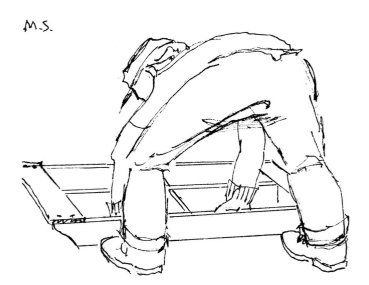

gunny sack, a board to bridge the ditch, a pair of work gloves, a can of Udder-eze to put on his hands to keep them from cracking, and perhaps a hose. Most of these things can be found at the local feed store. He also will need a 1 x 4, 30 inches long or longer for leveling the mud off his form, and a couple of masonry trowels.

The ground prepared, tools all handy, he wets the adobe form, lays it on the ground where he wishes to start his row of new adobes, and calls out "adobe". A helper is ready with a wheelbarrowful of mud, and as the adobe maker guides the adobe into all four sections of the form, the helper holds the wheelbarrow tipped so that the mud slips neatly and cleanly into the forms. The wheelbarrow, too, is wet and clean before it is filled or refilled.

The helper who stayed at the pit has been enlarging the working area of the pit, working toward a new mound which will be ready to have its crater filled with water just before they leave for the night. He stands for a moment of rest before helping to refill the wheelbarrow. The adobe they have prepared will make 250 to 300 adobes, and that will be all three men can make in a day.

The wheelbarrow is filled for a second spilling into the form. As soon as this is done, the adobe maker pats and pushes the mud into all corners and tightly against the edges of the form. Then he takes his 1 x 4 and scrapes the excess mud from the top of the form. If there are any low spots, he uses the excess mud to fill in such places. He then lifts his form, with a gentle backward, forward, side to side movement, until it is free of the newly formed adobes. The form will probably come off so cleanly that it will not have to be washed each time it is used.

Without undue haste, the work goes pretty fast, and no time is lost between the different operations. The adobe maker knows just the right time to go to the ditch or tub to wash his form with plenty of water and a piece of sacking. His helpers are conscious of his movements so that when he is ready for mud, there is a wheelbarrowful ready.

When his line of adobes stretches out to about 30 feet, he begins a new row, leaving room to walk between rows lying neatly side by side.

28

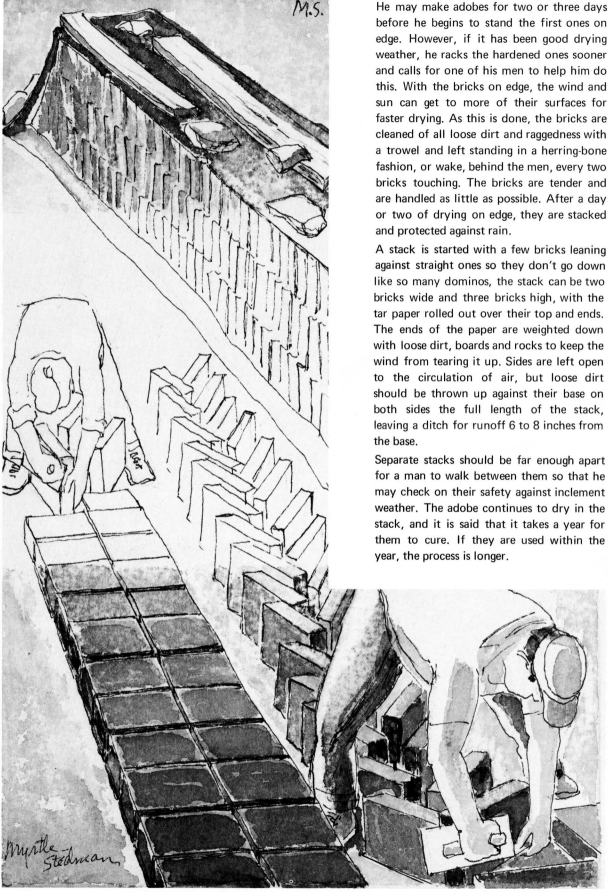

He may make adobes for two or three days before he begins to stand the first ones on edge. However, if it has been good drying weather, he racks the hardened ones sooner and calls for one of his men to help him do this. With the bricks on edge, the wind and sun can get to more of their surfaces for faster drying. As this is done, the bricks are cleaned of all loose dirt and raggedness with a trowel and left standing in a herring-bone fashion, or wake, behind the men, every two bricks touching. The bricks are tender and are handled as little as possible. After a day or two of drying on edge, they are stacked and protected against rain.

A stack is started with a few bricks leaning against straight ones so they don't go down like so many dominos, the stack can be two bricks wide and three bricks high, with the tar paper rolled out over their top and ends. The ends of the paper are weighted down with loose dirt, boards and rocks to keep the wind from tearing it up. Sides are left open to the circulation of air, but loose dirt should be thrown up against their base on both sides the full length of the stack, leaving a ditch for runoff 6 to 8 inches from the base.

Separate stacks should be far enough apart for a man to walk between them so that he may check on their safety against inclement weather. The adobe continues to dry in the stack, and it is said that it takes a year for them to cure. If they are used within the year, the process is longer.

Laying the Adobes

How many adobes the adobe maker will make and have in his stack for the building of his or your house will depend on how the adobes are to be laid into walls. In the old houses you will, as a rule, find thicker walls than in the newer houses, and practically all of the inside partitions will be of adobe instead of frame. This tends to soften the spoken word and make a more substantial and enduring adobe. The first drawing shows how 10 x 14-inch adobes are laid so that the wall is the thickness of the width of the adobe. This method is sometimes used for partition walls, but 10 inches is not considered thick enough for an outside wall. The second drawing shows how the adobes are laid to get a wall that is the thickness of the long dimension of the adobe. This method is often used for an outside wall if the wall is not to be more than 12 feet high. This drawing also shows how a string and level are used to keep the wall straight. A plumb bob is used when the wall gets higher. The third drawing shows the pattern of a 20-inch wall when 10 x 14-inch adobes are used. The thicker walls, 20 inches or more, are used for first floor walls of two-story houses or for a look of timelessness.

10" Wall

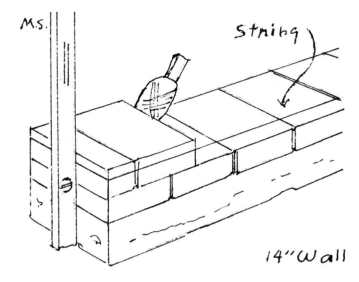

String

14" Wall

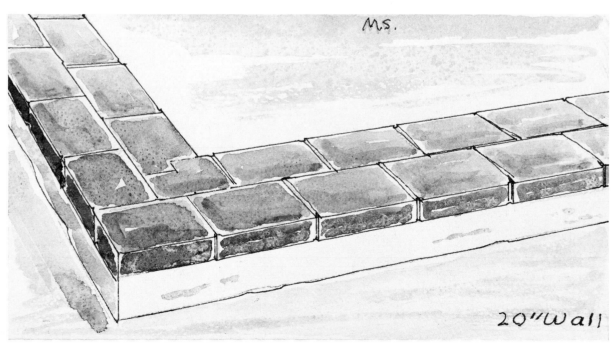

20" Wall

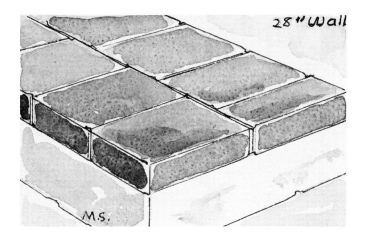

28" Wall

M.S.

You can easily see how a 28-inch wall is built by laying two adobes the long way end to end for width and with the joints staggered. You also can see how this staggering sometimes makes it necessary to use a half brick. The small second drawing shows an easy way to check corners. If a corner is square, 8 feet from the corner one way and 6 feet from the corner the other way, have a diagonal of 10 feet between those two points. The masons usually use some such check before the adobe mortar has set so that they can move the adobes in or out to comply with this check. Any adjustment that is made is made in relation to checks on all corners and in relation to the existing foundations. The third drawing shows two courses exhibiting the bonding method that takes place for a 24-inch wall. Other combinations could be used, but the builder has to have the picture clearly in mind so that he can know how wide to make his foundations and so he can figure how many adobes he will need. To find out how many adobes he needs, he will figure the adobe unit length or lengths (end or otherwise) as it appears in the wall, times the overall length of such wall, times the number of 4-inch courses it will take to reach the desired height of wall.

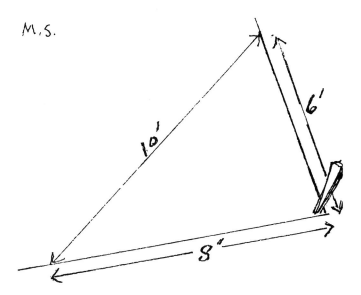

M.S.

10'   6'   8"

M.S.

24" Wall

Because of cutting, breakage and waste, window and door openings will not need to be accounted for in his counting unless the openings are significant (quite large).

THE MORTAR is made from the same type of ground the adobes were made. It is screened through a 1/4-inch wire mesh and mixed with water in a mud or mortar box. No straw is needed. The mud should not be too thin or too stiff but should slip easily from a wet shovel and not curl when it is troweled. The mortar will vary in thickness from 1/2-inch to 1 inch as it is spread out for the adobes to be laid onto it. The mason does not butter an adobe before it is laid as he does bricks, and does not fill in the joints between adobes with mortar. Small pieces of adobe are sometimes buttered before they are put into place. To handle mortar easily, an experienced man will keep his tools clean and leave them clean to dry overnight.

NAILING BLOCKS of 2 x 6 or wider should be built into the walls at window and door openings so that frames can be nailed to them. The blocks should be built in where any nailing to the walls is to take place, such as where stud partitions are to meet the adobe wall or where cabinets are to be fastened.

Metal lath should be tacked to both sides of the blocks so that they will be held securely by the mortar. Wood and adobe tend to shrink from one another, and if lath is not used, the blocks can become loose. In starting each new course, an adobe man works from openings and from corners so that he can take particular care that his openings will be true and his corners well bonded. Then, he fills in between.

STRAIGHT WALLS are accomplished by working from the outside, keeping weeping mortar scraped off and troweled smooth so that a level can be used. Adobes are set to, but not touching, string that is stretched for the courses to follow.

LINTELS are the wooden members that are placed above window and door openings or any other opening that is to appear in the wall. They carry a load of adobes and vigas (beams) so they should be heavy enough to make a sound bed to carry such a load, and they should rest a minimum of 8 inches on the wall beyond the opening at both sides. These members should not be less than 4 inches narrower than the thickness of the wall, and they are set on edge, not flat. In the illustration, the adobe man has used twin 6 x 8's with a 1-inch board in between, centered on the wall, and he has 12 inches resting on the wall at both sides of the opening.

VIGAS are beams, sometimes just round timbers with only the bark peeled off. They are especially nice in the Pueblo Indian Style house. The man in the small illustration is using a draw knife for dressing a viga. Where there are knots, he will use an axe, an adz or a hatchet to smooth off protrusions. Vigas must be chosen so that they are heavy enough to carry the weight of the ceiling material and whatever insulation is used. On an old house, you might find several inches of dirt being used for insulation, and even the lighter weight pumice that is used proves a weight problem to be considered. You may find 10 or 12-inch vigas on 30-inch centers in the old houses, and where we can, we use old methods to bring the substantial feeling of the old houses into the new one being built. Since the small end of the viga usually extends a foot or so to the outside and is exposed to the weather, it is well, too, to have a good sized viga to begin with. In the old houses, the protruding ends of the vigas were hollowed out to form a canale where one was needed to carry water from the roof. Even today a canale is usually supported by a viga. The lower drawing shows a viga being carried as they are when only manpower is available.

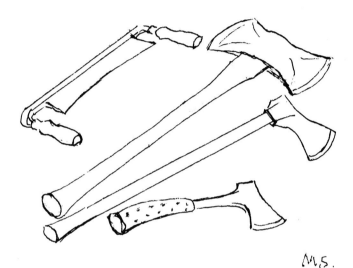

Another centuries old, manpowered device is shown here. One end of each of the two ropes is held while the other end is reeled in, guided by men below, to roll the viga up the inclined logs to the wall tops.

PLATES, either of 2-inch lumber or of reinforced poured cement several inches thick, should be laid on top of the walls to receive the vigas and to distribute their weight. Sometimes they are level from wall to wall and slope for drainage is gained by the graduated size of the viga.

CENTERING OF THE VIGAS is done and the vigas leveled, then the spaces between vigas are filled in with adobes.

THE CEILING DECK goes on, and another course of adobes is laid.

THE ROOFING MATERIAL is flashed over a wood cant strip, then over this course. Another course of adobes may go on, topped with 2 to 2-1/2 inches of mud, rounded to shed the water.

THE PARAPET WALL may be of kilned brick instead of adobe and mud, if squared, adzed or milled beams are used instead of round vigas and if the house is to be the more formal Spanish-Colonial type which uses other milled woodwork, such as window and door frames, baseboard and floors. Kilned brick also may be used if brick is used elsewhere for patios, foundations, fountains and walks.

35

FINISHING. After the last adobes are laid, there are a lot of things that need to be done before the plastering. Doors are hung, windows installed, and some of the trim is put in place so that the plaster can be finished up to it. Some places in the adobe work will need filling in, others rounded off. Wood beam ends are to be covered with metal lath where they are to be plastered over. Electrical wiring and plumbing channels are mudded in. Outside there is usually very little of this to be done. Most unevenness and channeling occurs inside under roof and cover where it is less serious during the building process.

Holes built into the foundation so that rainfall could escape before the roof went on can now be filled in. There is outside grading to do so that the men will know how far down to plaster, and inside floor levels must be established and floors laid. All installations should be checked to see that they are in place so there will be no breaking or channeling into the walls after the plastering is done.

All these things a good builder will know about and take in his stride. It is only hoped that this has been interesting and helpful in understanding the work and care that is involved in the building of an adobe house. The illustration shows the simple rope and pulley arrangement used to get heavy buckets of mud to roof level, and the wooden scaffolding so commonly used by the men. If they are plastering with adobe, the first coat will have straw in it, the second will be tempered with sand.

For more about plastering, see an earlier reference. Two things might be added to this. First, when wire mesh or metal lath is used, the twist of the wire and the cup of the lath will support the wet plaster without undue sagging if it is put on horizontally. Second, the hold of the cement-coated nail is superior to that of the common nail in adobe.

Indian Bread

Since this article first appeared in 1959, I have secured an original bread recipe from Alma Concha, also of Taos Pueblo. The recipe has been used for many years in making the delicious bread so sought after during feast days and other special occasions.

25 lbs. flour	4 cups water
1 pkg. yeast	1 handful salt
	2 lbs. lard

If making full recipe, mix dough in two batches. Begin by soaking yeast in water. While soaking, work salt and lard into flour. Add yeast and water mixture to flour mixture, adding more water as needed until dough is soft and springy. All mixing should be done with hands. Knead only as necessary. When well mixed, put dough in a large, greased container (a plastic 10-gallon trash can is adequate) and let dough rise overnight. Early the next morning, burn wood in the oven to heat it for baking. In the meantime, shape dough into small, round loafs and place them in tin pie pans. When the fire in the oven has burned down, mop oven out and test heat by using corn husks. Place corn husks in oven. If they burn, oven is too hot. If they brown, oven is right for baking. Use wooden paddle to insert bread in oven and seal for baking.

The Indian Oven

The horno *is an integral part of adobe architecture that has been overlooked for lack of knowledge and expertise. We are reprinting my article from the August 1969 issue of* New Mexico Magazine, *which to our knowledge is the only material on the subject printed in the Southwest. It carries no guarantee of the aquisition of expertise on the reader's part but does hope to convey the knowledge of "How to Make an Horno".*

It was at the Taos Pueblo on St. Geronimo Day when I was full of good food cooked in the Concha family's *horno* that Eva promised, "We come to your ranch and get some fruit and build for you a *horno*, and you see how we make it."

The fruit was ripe, the cottonwoods were golden in the sun and the mountains were getting their first coat of snow when Eva and John came early one Friday morning. I had 30 adobe bricks and a pile of rock waiting. We chose a high place in the yard. There Eva made a circular bed of rock on the ground, 44 inches in diameter.

M.S.

myrtle stedman

John mixed water with the dry earth in his wheelbarrow. Eva tested it with her trowel and said, "I like this adobe." John shoveled the mix from the wheelbarrow onto Eva's bed of rock. Then they laid 10 adobe bricks on this in the manner shown on the floor plan. Two adobe bricks were cut in a pie-shape to fit the space to form the curve at the back. The eleventh adobe on the floor plan was not laid at this time. They filled in between the adobe bricks so that they would stay in place. The diameter at this point was 38 inches. Rock and adobe protruded around the edges a couple of inches.

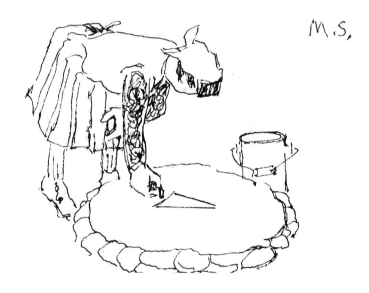

On top of the adobe bricks they placed adobe mix. This time Eva troweled it out smooth over the bricks. The center of this would be the floor of the oven. From the last of the mix, John shoveled onto the platform around its outer edges a mountainous range of adobe 6 inches in width. They set six adobe bricks on edge on this ring of adobe mud, leaving a gap before the hearth the length of an adobe. The bricks were set leaning slightly inward. Eva pulled the mud up tight against the bottom of the bricks and John filled in between the abutting ends.

This is where they would ordinarily leave it to completely set before going on with the building of the wall. We only took a coffee break. Eva looked at me and said, "At home just I make the *horno*, but for you John came also because we have to make it so fast . . . ."

38

M.S.

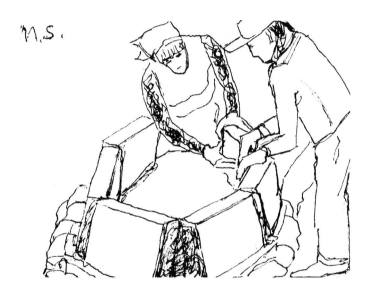

Together they started the second course of the wall. Two bricks were set on end on the two bricks on either side of the gap. John placed one and Eva placed the other. They leaned these together and placed a key between them at the top and mudded it in at the top and at the bottom where the bricks sat on the lower bricks of the wall. This made the doorway. John had previously made the key (a wedge 10 inches long cut from an adobe brick) and he was now cutting another one.

Eva plastered with adobe that had fine pieces of straw mixed into it now. She used her hand and she kept the floor clean while doing this. John added two more adobe bricks to the second course, one on one side of the *horno* and the other on the other side. These were placed on edge and mudded to their neighbor. Directly in the back he stood two on end side by side, leaned them forward slightly and mudded them in place. This second course gave the structure a jagged appearance.

Three bricks remained to be locked into place. Two 10-inch ones were leaned together at their top and keyed; the third brick went directly in the back, leaned to touch the keyed 10-inch ones and mudded in place. The walls and the dome were complete. This interlocking pattern can be more easily understood in the drawings.

Keys

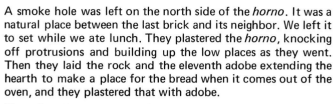

A smoke hole was left on the north side of the *horno*. It was a natural place between the last brick and its neighbor. We left it to set while we ate lunch. They plastered the *horno*, knocking off protrusions and building up the low places as they went. Then they laid the rock and the eleventh adobe extending the hearth to make a place for the bread when it comes out of the oven, and they plastered that with adobe.

They found a round rock for the smoke hole and a flagstone for the door, and it was finished. It was 2 o'clock and it began to rain. We covered the oven with a couple of shower curtains and ran for the barn.

John said, "When you are going to make bread you build a fire in the *horno* early in the morning. When it has burned down to ashes you tie a wet cloth onto the end of a stick and sweep all of the ashes out until the floor is clean. Then you put your pans of bread in on the floor; close up the door and the smoke hole and let it bake. On the inside of the door and the smoke hole rock you lay a damp cloth and you lay it back around the rocks to close up the cracks to keep the heat in."

For baking turkey you leave the coals in the oven and set your turkey in a pan on the coals. The coals are all around the pan too, and you mud up the smoke hole and the cracks around the door. You do not open it for 4-1/2 hours. It cooks in its own juices and is delicious.

Fruitwood is best for the fire. It should be 1 to 2 inches thick and about 18 inches long. The Indians really do a neat job of putting it in, placing one stick in at a time until it is full.

We filled John's truck with fruit from my bins and they went home to bake bread for a wedding.

Smoke hole

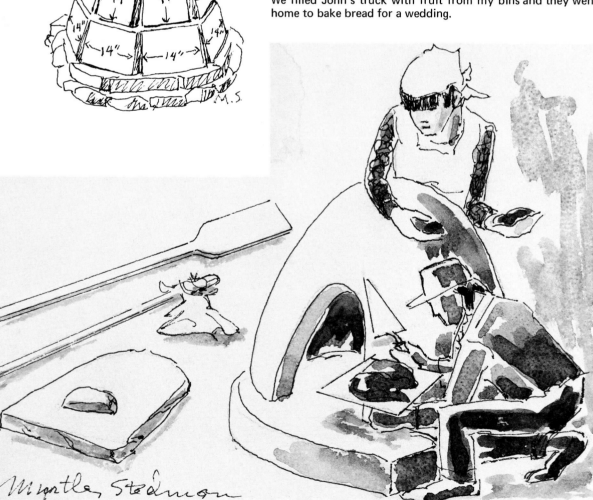

Myrtle Stedman

40

Wilfred Stedman

WILFRED STEDMAN — a native of Liverpool, England, emigrated with his family to Canada while still a boy and became apprenticed to an architectural firm in Winnipeg, and altogether spent 20 years in this work. He studied at St. Mary's College (Winnipeg), The Minneapolis Institute of Fine Arts, the Art Students League (New York) and the University of Bescanson in France. He served in the Engineer Corps during World War I on General Pershing's staff. He was the Director of Industrial Arts at the Broadmoor Art Academy before moving to Houston as a free lance painter and illustrator.

MYRTLE L. STEDMAN — born in Charleston, Illinois, and brought up in Houston, Texas. As the daughter of a builder, she absorbed facts and knowledge about design and building along with the more usual three R's. She studied at the Houston Museum of Fine Arts School with Frederic Browne and with Ward Lockwood.

After their marriage, Myrtle and Wilfred conducted the Stedman School of Art. In 1934 they moved to New Mexico, building a home and studio in Tesuque, a small village just north of Santa Fe. In New Mexico they continued their art careers and became interested in both building adobe houses and restoring adobe homes.

Wilfred, who died in 1950, was the Art Editor for the *New Mexico Magazine* for sixteen years. During World War II he worked with Kruger & Associates, architects on the Los Alamos Project.

The Stedmans' two sons shared their parents' interest in adobe construction and many projects became family activities. After Wilfred's death, Myrtle continued to build and remodel adobe homes. Known as "An Artist in Adobe," she has held a contractor's license for many years. In addition, she has continued to paint and exhibit her art work.

Myrtle L. Stedman

Photograph by Beverly Gile